Hey ! Solar System

Let's go.

JUPITER
URENUS
EARTH
MERCURY
MARS
VENUS
SATURN
NEPTU
SUN

SUN

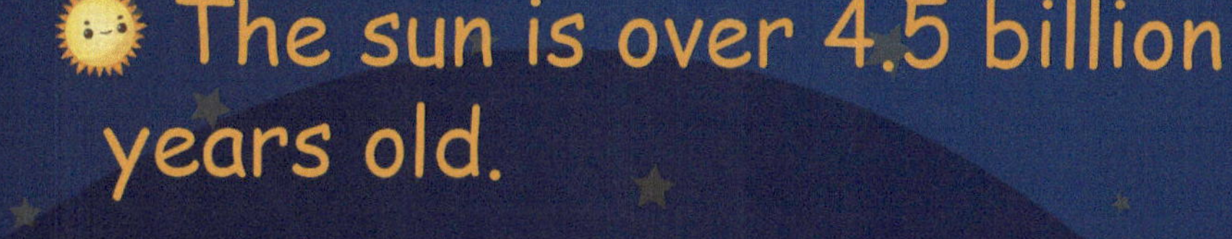

The sun is a huge hot star.

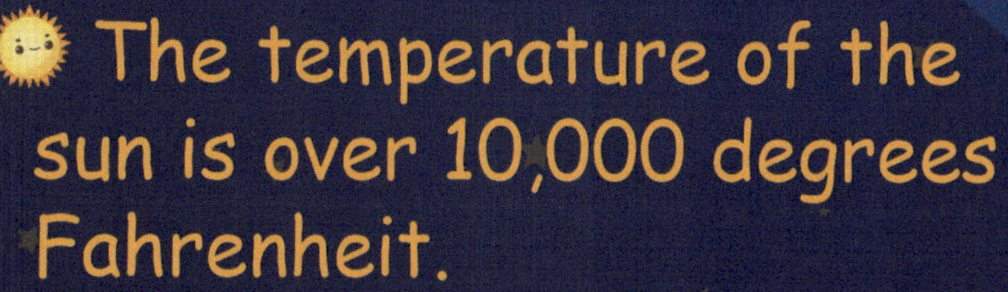

The sun is over 4.5 billion years old.

The temperature of the sun is over 10,000 degrees Fahrenheit.

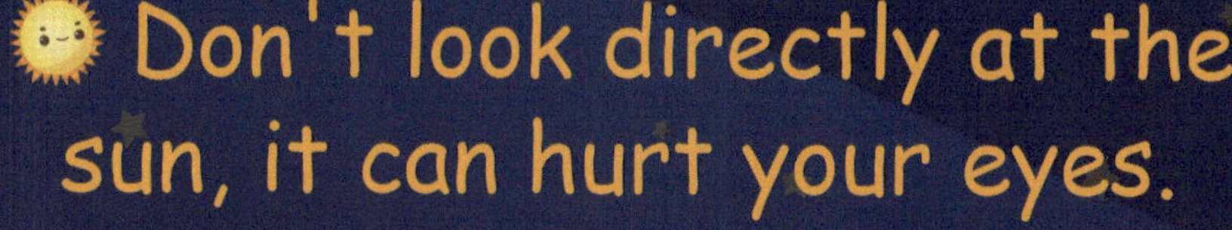

Don't look directly at the sun, it can hurt your eyes.

MERCURY

- Mercury is the smallest planet in the solar System.

- Mercury is about the size of Earth's moon.

- Mercury takes 88 days to orbit the sun.

VENUS

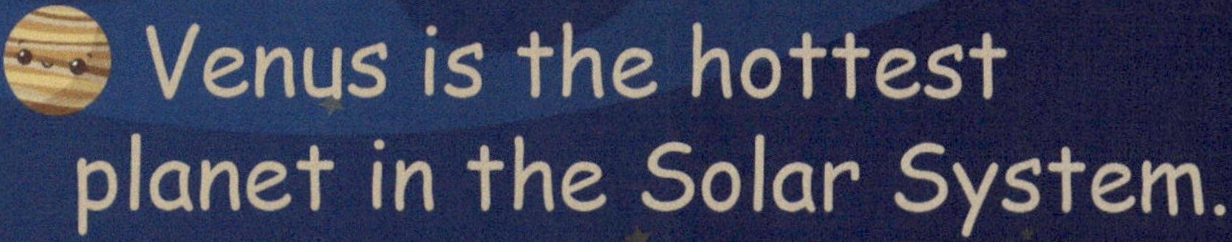 Venus is the hottest planet in the Solar System.

 Venus is about the size of Earth.

Venus spins the opposite direction as Earth.

EARTH

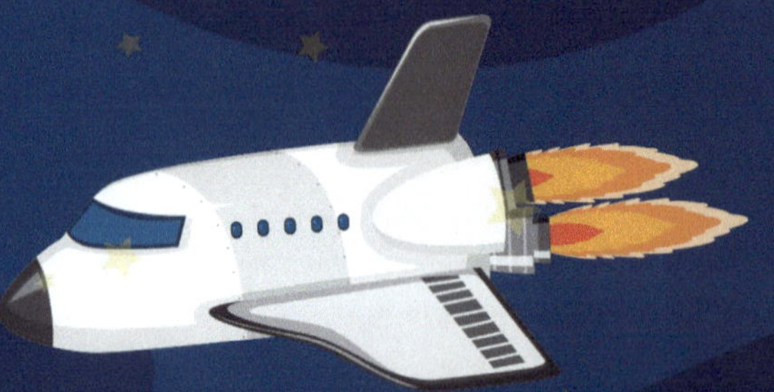

Earth is the only planet where life exists.

The Earth is orbited by one moon.

Earth is the third planet from the sun.

MARS

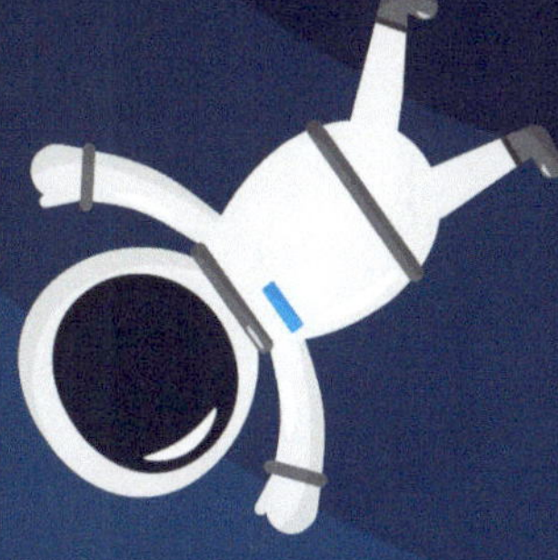

Mars has two moons named Phobos and Deimos.

Named after Roman god of war.

Mars has the tallest mountain in the Solar System.

Jupiter has 67 moons.

Jupiter is fastest spinning planet in the Solar System.

Jupiter has 4 sets of rings.

SATURN

 Saturn has 82 moons.

 Saturn has been visited by 4 spacecrafts.

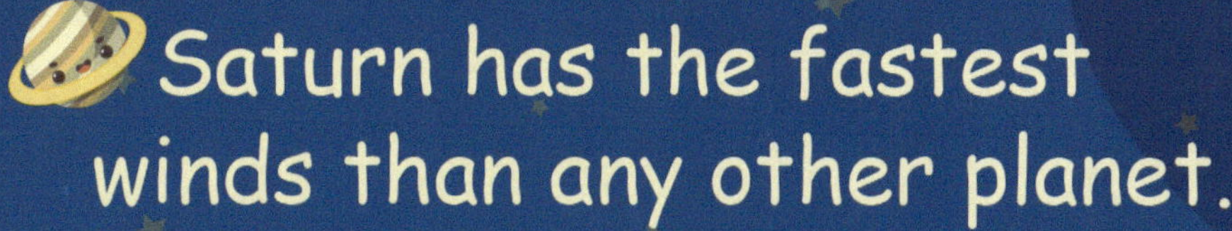 Saturn has the fastest winds than any other planet.

URANUS

- Uranus has 2 sets of very thin dark colored rings.

- Only one spacecarft has flown by Uranus.

- Uranus is nicknamed as the "Ice giant"

NEPTUNE

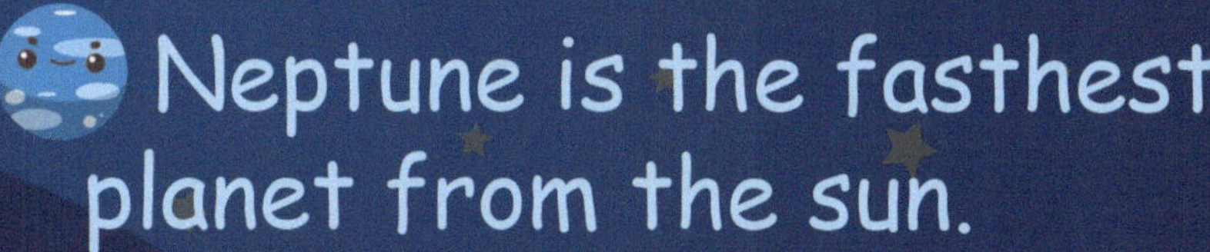
Neptune is the fasthest planet from the sun.

Neptune is named after the Roman god of the sea.

Neptune has 14 moons.

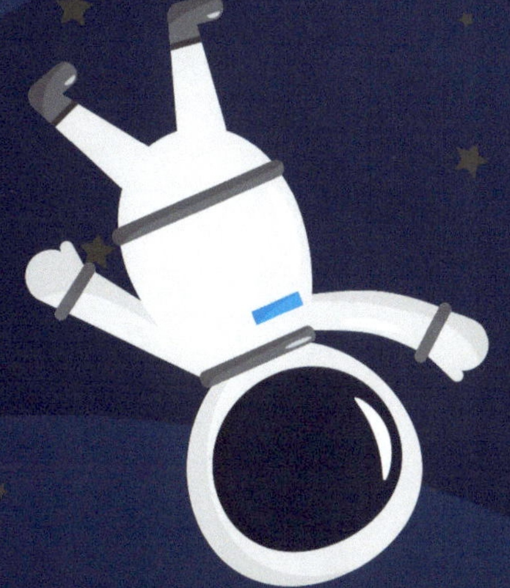

I am a huge
hot star.

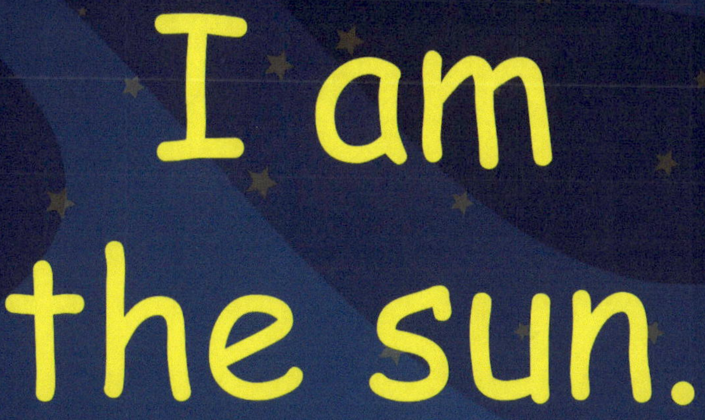

I am
the sun.

I am smallest planet in the Solar System.

I am
the mercury.

I am hottest planet in the Solar System.

I am
the venus.

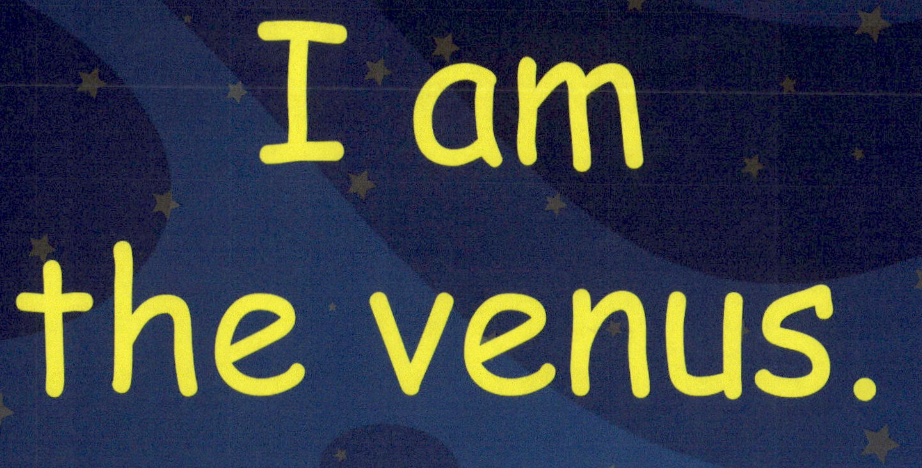

I am only planet where life exists.

I am
the earth.

Who am I?
I have two moons named Phobos and Deimos.

I am
the mars.

Who am I?

I am fastest spinning planet in the Solar System.

I am
the jupiter.

Who am I?
I have the fastest winds than any other planet.

I am
the saturn.

Who am I?
I have a nicknamed as the "Ice giant"

I am
the uranus.

I am farthest planet from the sun.

I am
the neptune.

Thank you